LOOKING AT
COUNTRIES

Looking at
ARGENTINA

Kathleen Pohl

Reading consultant: Susan Nations, M.Ed.,
author/literacy coach/consultant in literacy development

Gareth Stevens
Publishing

Please visit our Web site at **www.garethstevens.com**.
For a free color catalog describing **Gareth Stevens Publishing's** list
of high-quality books, call 1-800-542-2595 (USA) or 1-800-387-3178 (Canada).
Gareth Stevens Publishing's fax: 1-877-542-2596

Library of Congress Cataloging-in-Publication Data

Pohl, Kathleen.
   Looking at Argentina / Kathleen Pohl.
      p. cm. — (Looking at countries)
   Includes bibliographical references and index.
   ISBN-10: 0-8368-8765-4   ISBN-13: 978-0-8368-8765-5 (lib. bdg.)
   ISBN-10: 0-8368-8772-7   ISBN-13: 978-0-8368-8772-3 (softcover)
   1. Argentina—Juvenile literature. I. Title.
  F2808.2.P64   2008
  982—dc22   2007027671

This edition first published in 2008 by
Gareth Stevens Publishing
A Weekly Reader® Company
1 Reader's Digest Road
Pleasantville, NY 10570-7000 USA

Copyright © 2008 by Gareth Stevens, Inc.

Senior Managing Editor: Lisa M. Guidone
Senior Editor: Barbara Bakowski
Creative Director: Lisa Donovan
Designer: Tammy West
Photo Researcher: Kimberly Babbitt

Photo credits: (t=top, c=center, b=bottom)
Cover Nicolas Russell/Getty Images; title page Pablo Corral Vega/Corbis; p. 4 Jon Hicks/Corbis;
p. 6 Michael Lewis/Corbis; p. 7t Joseph Sohm/Corbis; p. 7b Fulvio Roiter/Corbis; p. 8 David R. Frazier/
Alamy; p. 9t Therin-Weise/Arco Images/Peter Arnold; p. 9b Michele Falzone/JAI/Corbis; p. 10t SuperStock;
p. 10b Marianna Day Massey/Corbis; p. 11t Sarah Murray/Masterfile; p. 11b Juncal/Alamy; p. 12 Achim Pol/
Peter Arnold; p. 13 Achim Pol/Peter Arnold; p. 14 SuperStock; p. 15t Masterfile; p. 15b Natacha Pisarenko/
AP Images; p. 16 T. Ozonas/Masterfile; p. 17. SuperStock; p. 18 Wolfgang Kaehler/Corbis; p. 19t Brand X/
SuperStock; p. 19b Eric Ghost/Alamy; p. 20t Alison Wright/Corbis; p. 20b John E. Kelly/Jupiter; p. 21 John Hicks/
Corbis; p. 22 Neil Beer/Corbis; p. 23t Tim Brakemeier/dpa/Corbis; p. 23b Hubert Stadler/Corbis; p. 24 Chad Ehlers/
Jupiter; p. 25t Angelo Cavalli/Getty Images; p. 25b Paul Souders/Corbis; p. 26 Comstock/Jupiter; p. 27t Getty Images;
p. 27c SuperStock; p. 27b Robert Frerck/Getty Images

Printed in the United States of America

1 2 3 4 5 6 7 8 9 10 09 08 07

Contents

Words that appear in the glossary are printed in **boldface** type the first time they occur in the text.

Where Is Argentina?

Argentina is the second-largest country on the **continent** of South America. Only Brazil is larger. Argentina shares a border with five countries. Chile is to the west, and Bolivia and Paraguay lie to the north. Argentina's northeastern neighbors are Brazil and Uruguay. On the east, Argentina borders the Atlantic Ocean.

Argentina makes up a big part of South America. Argentina is the second-largest country on the continent, after Brazil.

The president of Argentina lives and works in the Casa Rosada ("Pink House") in Buenos Aires.

Buenos Aires (bway-nohs EYE-rays), the capital, is the largest city in Argentina. This busy port is a modern city, like New York or Paris. It has government centers, apartment houses, offices, museums, and parks.

Argentina also includes half of the island of Tierra del Fuego (tee-EHR-ah dell FWAY-goh) in the south.

Did you know?

The town of Ushuaia (oo-SWIGH-ah) is on Tierra del Fuego. It is one of the southernmost towns in the world.

This map shows all the places that are mentioned in this book.

The Landscape

Argentina has grassy **plains** and high mountains. It also has waterfalls and icy **glaciers**.

The lowlands in the north include two areas known as the Gran Chaco and Mesopotamia. The Gran Chaco is dry much of the year. The area is covered with low trees and shrubs. It lies between the Andes Mountains and the Paraná River. Between the Paraná and Uruguay rivers is Mesopotamia. That is an area of farmland, grasslands, and swampy forests.

Did you know?

Aconcagua (ah-kohn-KAH-gwah), in the Andes, is the highest mountain in North and South America.

Aconcagua is a volcano that is no longer active. Long ago it was higher, but its top has worn away.

This waterfall is really a group of hundreds of separate falls. People hike on trails or ride in boats to see the falls.

Big cattle ranches cover much of the grassy plains of the Pampas.

In the middle of Argentina are the **Pampas**. These large, grassy plains have some of the best farmland in the world.

The Andes rise along the western border of Argentina. In the south is Patagonia, a high, windy plain.

Weather and Seasons

Did you know that summer happens at different times in different parts of the world? In the United States, summer is in June, July, and August. In Argentina, summer is in December, January, and February, when most of the United States has cold weather.

In northern Argentina, the average temperature in January is about 80° Fahrenheit (27° Celsius). It is cooler in the south—about 60° F (16° C).

Many people enjoy visiting Mar del Plata. It has beautiful sandy beaches on the Atlantic coast.

Thick forests cover the northeastern part of Mesopotamia.

The Perito Moreno is one of about three hundred icy glaciers in Argentina.

Mesopotamia, in the northeast, is hot and wet. More than 60 inches (1,520 millimeters) of rain fall each year. The Gran Chaco is mostly hot and dry. Still, heavy rains in summer can cause flooding.

The coastal area near Buenos Aires is warm and damp in summer and cool in winter. The central Pampas have dry winters and hot summers.

In winter, snow falls in the high peaks of the Andes. In parts of Patagonia, it is so cold that glaciers can be seen year round.

Argentine People

About thirty-nine million people live in Argentina. People who settled there came from countries in Europe. Most of the settlers came from Spain and Italy. Others came from Austria, England, France, and Germany.

Some Argentines are **mestizos** (meh-STEE-zohs). Their **ancestors** were European and American Indian. About fifty thousand native Indians live in the countryside of Argentina.

Some traditional native families live in villages in Argentina.

Argentines celebrate at festivals. They wear costumes and perform folk dances.

Argentina's cities and towns have many churches. This church is in Luján.

This newspaper stand in Buenos Aires sells papers in different languages.

Almost all Argentines speak Spanish. That is the country's main language. Many also speak a second language, such as Italian or English.

Most people in Argentina are Roman Catholic. Some others practice Protestant or Jewish religions.

School and Family

Argentine children from ages six to fourteen must go to school. The school year starts in March and ends in December. Children go to school either in the morning or in the afternoon.

Students learn math, science, language arts, and social studies. They also take part in music and dance and play soccer, rugby, and basketball.

Did you know?

There are no public school buses in Argentina. Children in some areas ride to school on horses.

Students in Argentina learn math, as well as science, languages, and history. More schools are in big cities than in the countryside.

After school, many children play sports. Soccer is a favorite game.

Only a small number of students finish high school and go on to college. Boys and girls who don't finish school often go to work in the community or on farms.

Most families are close-knit, with children, parents, and grandparents living together. They often celebrate birthdays and holidays with large family gatherings.

Country Life

In Argentina, one in ten people lives in the country. Most people live in the Pampas. Some of them work on big **estancias** (eh-STAHNTS-yahs), or ranches. Wealthy ranch owners hire cowboys to look after cattle or sheep. The cowboys are called **gauchos**. The owners rent land to farmers, who grow wheat, corn, and soybeans. Usually, people who work on estancias live there, too. Children may go to school on the ranches.

On some ranches, gauchos wear hats with wide brims. They tuck their loose pants into high boots.

Modern estancias have big herds of sheep and cattle.

Did you know?

Long ago, gauchos roamed freely across the Pampas. They hunted wild horses and cattle.

People grow grapes on vines in the Piedmont area.

In the Piedmont area, farmers grow sugarcane and corn. They also grow cotton and grapes.

Few people live in the Andes Mountains or on the dry plains of Patagonia. Most of the people who live there raise sheep for wool.

City Life

Since the 1930s, many people have moved to cities to look for jobs. Today, nine of ten people live and work in cities and towns. Most large cities are on the Pampas. The land there is flat, and the weather is mild. Most towns and cities have a main square called a **plaza**.

Buses, taxis, and cars crowd the streets of Argentina's big cities.

This avenue in Buenos Aires is one of the world's widest streets.

About fourteen million people live in and around Buenos Aires. It is one of the world's largest cities. Buenos Aires has wide streets, tall buildings, and busy plazas. It is the center of government, banking, business, and the arts.

Argentina's second-largest city, Córdoba, has many **factories**. Rosario is a busy port city.

Many Argentines own cars. City streets are crowded, so most people travel by bus or taxi. Many of Argentina's big cities have modern airports.

Argentine Houses

In cities, many people live in tall, modern apartment buildings or in large, old brick houses. Others live in houses with small yards. In the country, large houses on estancias are often painted white. The rooms are built around an inner patio, or courtyard.

Did you know?

A large country house on a ranch is called a **hacienda** (hah-see-EN-dah).

A hacienda is the main house on a large ranch or farm. It has adobe walls and a tile roof.

Many houses in the countryside are built of **adobe**, or sun-dried clay. Most houses have tile roofs. Some poor people in the countryside live in huts with dirt floors and straw roofs.

These houses are made of metal and wood. They are painted a rainbow of colors.

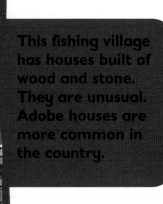

This fishing village has houses built of wood and stone. They are unusual. Adobe houses are more common in the country.

Argentine Food

Do you like hamburgers or steak? Both of those foods are beef. People in Argentina eat a lot of beef. Some people eat beef at every meal. Argentines like to barbecue beef, or cook it outdoors over an open fire.

Other favorite foods include stews and filled pies called **empanadas**. Pasta and pizza are also popular.

People serve maté in the dried shell of a fruit. They sip the drink through a straw.

Empanadas are pies stuffed with meat, eggs, vegetables, or fruit.

Argentines often eat at sidewalk cafés.

Argentines like to drink **maté** (MAH-tay). It is made from the leaves and stems of a tree. Many people drink maté in the afternoon with sandwiches and desserts.

People in the cities like to eat at cafés and restaurants. They enjoy trying foods from different countries.

Did you know?

Maté is the national drink of Argentina. People make the drink by pouring boiling water over the leaves and stems of a holly tree.

21

At Work

Argentines work in banks, schools, hospitals, and restaurants. Many people have jobs in tourism and the arts. Some own small businesses.

Argentina's factories make most of the nation's food and clothing. In Buenos Aires, people work in meatpacking plants and leather companies. Factories in Córdoba make cars and trains. In Rosario, many people work in the oil business. Others work in chemical plants or in shipping.

Did you know?

Oil fields in Patagonia and the Piedmont produce enough oil for almost all of Argentina's needs.

Workers remove oil from the ground. Then the oil travels through pipes and tanks.

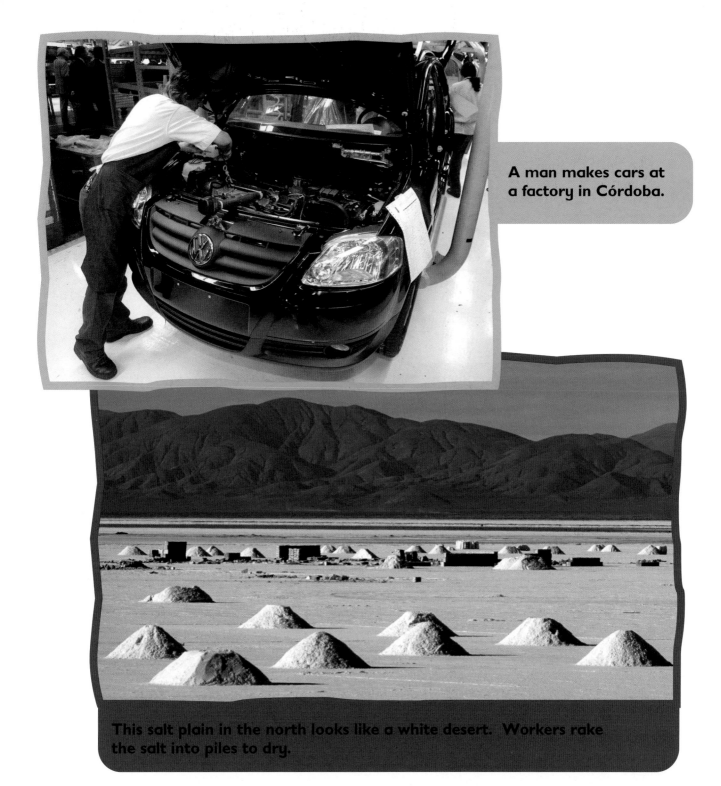

A man makes cars at a factory in Córdoba.

This salt plain in the north looks like a white desert. Workers rake the salt into piles to dry.

Farming is an important business in Argentina. Beef, corn, and wheat are shipped from Argentina to countries around the world. Other important farm products are fruits, cotton, potatoes, sugarcane, wool, and tea.

Having Fun

Argentina's national sport is soccer. People of all ages enjoy playing it and watching it. Another favorite sport is **pato**. That is a kind of basketball on horseback. Polo, boating, and car and horse racing are popular, too.

Crowds of fans watch soccer teams play Argentina's favorite sport.

The dance style called the tango began in Argentina.

People watch whales off Argentina's southern coast.

People enjoy relaxing at sandy beaches, such as the ones in Mar del Plata. They bike and hike in national parks. In winter, they ski in the mountains. Each year, many people visit Glaciers National Park in Patagonia. The park has forty-seven big glaciers.

Argentines like to read, watch television, see movies, and listen to music at nightclubs and discos. They love dancing the **tango**. It is the national dance of Argentina. In big cities, people enjoy operas, ballets, and concerts.

25

Argentina: The Facts

- Argentina is a **republic**. Its official name is Argentine Republic.

- Argentina's president is the **head of state** and the leader of the government. The president is elected to serve for four years.

- Argentina is divided into parts called **provinces**. A province is similar to a state and is led by a governor.

- About thirty-nine million people live in Argentina. Most of them live in the northern half of the country.

- Citizens of Argentina who are eighteen years old or older must vote in the country's elections.

The Argentine flag has two blue stripes and one white stripe. The yellow sun in the middle is a symbol of Argentina's freedom. Argentina was ruled by Spain for almost three hundred years.

Argentine currency is called the **peso** (PAY-soh). People use both paper money and coins in Argentina.

Did you know?

Argentina is the eighth-largest country in the world.

The Plaza de Mayo is the main public square in Buenos Aires. Many tourists visit its famous buildings.

Glossary

adobe – sun-dried brick

ancestors – family members who lived in the past

continent – one of the main landmasses of Earth

empanadas – pies filled with meat, vegetables, or fruit

estancias – large cattle ranches in South America

factories – buildings where workers make goods

gauchos – cowboys of the South American plains

glaciers – large masses of ice that move slowly down a slope or valley or spread outward on a land surface

hacienda – a country house or the main building on a ranch in South America

head of state – the main representative of a country

maté – a tea-like drink made from the leaves of a holly tree that grows in South America

mestizos – people of mixed European and American Indian ancestry

Pampas – the large grassy plains in central Argentina that have good farmland

pamperos – strong, cold winds from the west or southwest that blow over the Pampas

pato – a sport played in Argentina where people on horseback try to toss a six-handled ball into a high basket

peso – Argentina's unit of money

plains – large areas of flat land

plaza – a square in a city or town

provinces – large divisions of a country

republic – a kind of government in which decisions are made by the people of the country and their representatives

tango – a slow ballroom dance that is the national dance of Argentina

Find Out More

Fact Monster: Argentina
www.factmonster.com/ipka/A0107288.html

FunTrivia: Argentina
www.funtrivia.com/en/Geography/Argentina-9979.html

KidsKonnect: Argentina
www.kidskonnect.com/Argentina/ArgentinaHome.html

Publisher's note to educators and parents: Our editors have carefully reviewed these Web sites to ensure that they are suitable for children. Many Web sites change frequently, however, and we cannot guarantee that a site's future contents will continue to meet our high standards of quality and educational value. Be advised that children should be closely supervised whenever they access the Internet.

My Map of Argentina

Photocopy or trace the map on page 31. Then write in the names of the countries, bodies of water, regions, islands, cities, mountains, and glaciers listed below.
(Look at the map on page 5 if you need help.)

After you have written in the names of all the places, find some crayons and color the map!

Countries
Argentina
Bolivia
Brazil
Chile
Paraguay
Uruguay

Bodies of Water
Atlantic Ocean
Paraná River
Uruguay River

Islands
Tierra del Fuego

Mountains and Glaciers
Andes Mountains
Aconcagua
Perito Moreno

Regions
Gran Chaco
Mesopotamia
Pampas
Patagonia
Piedmont

Cities and Towns
Buenos Aires
Córdoba
Luján
Mar del Plata
Rosario
Ushuaia

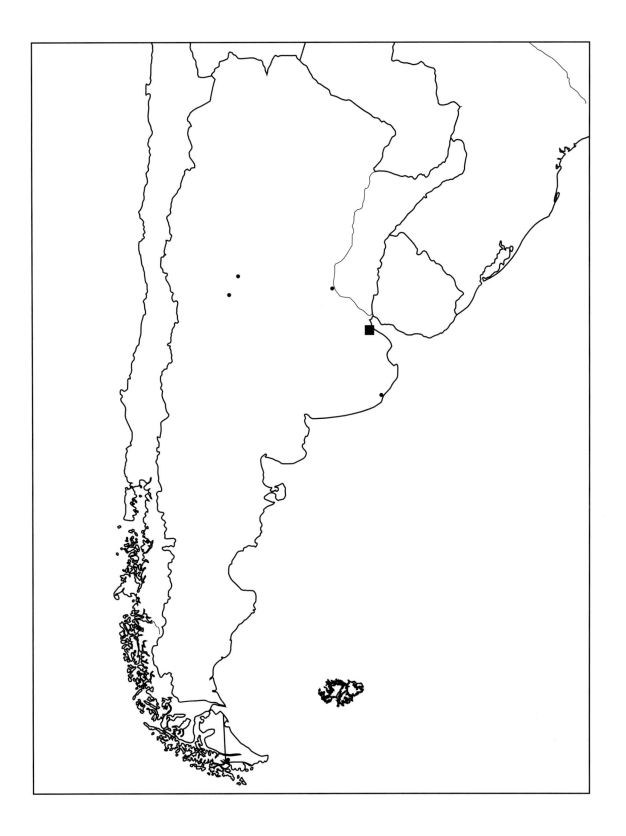

Index